THE MAGNIFICENT
❧ BOOK ❧
OF
DANGEROUS
ANIMALS

THE MAGNIFICENT

❧ BOOK ❧

OF

DANGEROUS
ANIMALS

ILLUSTRATED BY
Val Walerczuk

WRITTEN BY
Tom Jackson

weldon**owen**

Written by Tom Jackson
Illustrated by Val Walerczuk

weldon**owen**

Published by Weldon Owen Children's Books
An imprint of Weldon Owen International, L.P.
A subsidiary of Insight International, L.P.
PO Box 3088
San Rafael, CA 94912
www.insighteditions.com

Weldon Owen Children's Books:
Designed by Bryn Walls
Edited by Diana Craig
Assistant Editor: Pandita Geary
Art Director: Stuart Smith
Senior Production Manager: Greg Steffen
Publisher: Sue Grabham

Insight Editions:
Publisher: Raoul Goff

ISBN: 978-1-68188-869-9
Manufactured, printed
and assembled in China.
First printing, June 2022.
DRM0622
10 9 8 7 6 5 4 3 2

 # Introduction

Let's take a look at some magnificent—and dangerous—animals. All the creatures included in this book pose a threat to each other, to their prey, and often to us humans as well. They include the biggest and the toughest beasts out there, such as the polar bear and the Nile crocodile. However, danger does not always come through strength. Many deadly creatures use cunning, stealth, and powerful weapons. For example, the box jellyfish is a very flimsy creature that wafts through the oceans—but its sting can kill prey instantly, and a person in minutes.

Very often, the danger that animals pose to humans is accidental. The tiny mosquito is not trying to hurt us. In fact, it uses painkilling saliva so that we do not even feel its bite as it sucks our blood for dinner. However, the diseases that the mosquito spreads with its bites, such as malaria and dengue fever, kill hundreds of thousands of people each year—more than all the other dangerous animals in this book put together.

Fact file

Lives: India, Southeast Asia

Habitat: Forest

Length: 8–18 ft. (2.4–5.5 m)

Weight: 13 lb. (6 kg)

Lifespan: 17 years

Diet: Mainly snakes, also lizards, small mammals

The king cobra is one of the most venomous snakes around but also one of the shyest. If cornered, it will rear up and spread its hoodlike neck to give its famous warning. If you are in the way, you will get a bite laced with deadly venom.

The important thing to remember about wild animals is to be careful and respectful. If you leave them alone, they will generally leave you alone, too!

Contents

Lion

Panthera leo

Male lions are extremely territorial. They will defend their territory from other lions while guarding and protecting the cubs.

Male lions claim their territory by pacing and roaring. A lion's roar can be heard 3 miles (5 km) away.

When a new lion takes over a pride, he may kill any cubs not yet weaned.

Fact file

Lives: Africa (and one forest in India)

Habitat: Grassland

Length: 5–6.5 ft. (1.5–2 m)

Weight: 265–550 lb. (120–250 kg)

Lifespan: 10–14 years

Diet: Antelopes, zebras, wildebeest, giraffes, wild pigs

Adult lions have no natural predators and can bring down prey much larger than themselves, such as zebra and wildebeest.

A lion's stomach is very stretchy, so it can eat a quarter of its body weight in one meal—about 17 pounds (8 kg) of meat every day.

A lion's tongue is barbed and rough enough to lick raw meat off of a bone.

About 250 people are killed by lions every year.

Hippopotamus

Hippopotamus amphibius

Hippos are Africa's most dangerous mammal. They attack people who get too close to them, resulting in about 500 deaths a year.

Hippos have a bite stronger than a lion's, a tiger's, or a polar bear's. They fight over mates and territory and can chomp their teeth right through a person's body.

When annoyed, a hippo can charge at its enemy at speeds of up to 18 miles per hour (30 kph).

A hippo often yawns, but not because it is tired. It is showing other hippos how big its teeth are.

Fact file

Lives: Africa

Habitat: Rivers, lakes, freshwater wetlands

Length: 10–16.5 ft. (3–5 m)

Weight: 3,000–10,000 lb (1,400–4,500 kg)

Lifespan: 40–50 years

Diet: Grass, shoots, reeds

A hippo uses its tail to fling poo around. This spreads its smell so other animals know where it lives.

Hippos use water to stay cool during the day. At night, they come onto riverbanks to eat grass.

A hippo's skin is about 2.5 inches (6 cm) thick! The skin produces red liquid that works like sunscreen to protect against sunburn.

Box jellyfish

Chironex fleckeri

 The box jellyfish, also known as the sea wasp, is among the most toxic animals in the world.

 Its 60 tentacles are covered with about 5,000 tiny cells that sting. Altogether, they contain enough venom to kill 30 people.

 To deliver a fatal dose of venom, stingers from 20 feet (6 m) of tentacles need to touch a person. Each box jellyfish has nearly 600 feet (180 m) of tentacles.

 A sting from a box jellyfish is a medical emergency, but only 60 people have died from jellyfish attacks in the last 100 years.

Fact file

Lives: Indian and eastern Pacific oceans

Habitat: Coastal waters

Length: 10 ft. (3 m)

Weight: 4.5 lb. (2 kg)

Lifespan: 9 months

Diet: Fish and prawns

Sea turtles prey on box jellyfish, as they are unaffected by the venom.

Unlike other jellyfish, which drift along with the current, the box jellyfish is a strong swimmer.

Box jellyfish wrap their tentacles around their victims to inject toxins into the bloodstream. By killing its victims instantly, the jellyfish avoids damaging its fragile tentacles.

Western diamondback rattlesnake

Crotalus atrox

- The western diamondback rattlesnake is the deadliest snake in North America.

- This snake's famous rattle is made from the pieces of dried skin that are left behind when the snake sheds its outer layer.

- The rattle warns predators to stay away. It makes up to sixty clicks a second to create the frightening sound.

- In a tenth of a second, this snake can reach—and attack—an animal that is half of its own body length away.

- The snake injects its poison by biting. Its teeth can sometimes break off and stay in its prey, but they will grow back.

- Its powerful bite kills about 12 people every year.

Fact file

Lives: Western USA, Mexico

Habitat: Dry areas covered in shrubs

Length: 5–7 ft (1.5–2.1 m)

Weight: 4–15 lb (1.75–6.75 kg)

Lifespan: 25 years

Diet: Small mammals, birds, reptiles, amphibians

Grizzly bear

Ursus arctos horribilis

🐻 Grizzlies are powerful predators with a reputation as one of nature's most dangerous killing machines.

🐻 These bears are excellent swimmers and fast runners. They can run at up to 35 miles per hour (50 kph).

🐻 They have perfect eyesight and the best sense of smell of any land animal. They can smell seven times better than a bloodhound!

🐻 Grizzlies have a hump between their shoulders. This contains the huge muscles that move their front legs.

Fact file

Lives: North America

Habitat: Mountain forest

Length: 5.5–9 ft. (1.7–2.8 m)

Weight: 300–900 lb. (130–440 kg)

Lifespan: 25–30 years

Diet: Fruit, nuts, grass, roots, small rodents, birds, fish

- Grizzlies are highly intelligent and have excellent memories. Their memory is so sharp, they can remember hunting grounds they haven't visited in over 10 years.

- Grizzly bears will cover their leftover food with moss and grass. Chemicals in the moss stop the food from rotting.

- Despite being the biggest predator in North America, grizzly bears kill only, on average, three people each year.

Asian tiger mosquito

Aedes *albopictus*

The male mosquito eats pollen and nectar. The female mosquito needs richer food to grow her eggs, so she drinks blood from birds and mammals—including humans.

The female drives a needle-shaped mouthpart into skin to suck out blood. As she bites, she squirts in a little saliva, which may contain infectious diseases.

Females lay their eggs near a stagnant pool or running water, often near flowers.

Fact file

Lives: Mainly eastern Asia, Pacific islands

Habitat: Tropical and subtropical forests

Length: 0.1–0.4 in. (2–10 mm)

Wingspan: 0.1 in. (2.7 mm)

Lifespan: 40 days

Diet: Males, nectar; females, blood

The eggs of this mosquito are spreading around the world, transported in old rubber tires, bamboo, and other Asian plants.

In recent years, the tiger mosquito has spread from Asia to other parts of the world—to warm areas such as the Mediterranean, the southern USA, and Central America.

In Asia, the tiger mosquito carries chikungunya fever and dengue fever, and in South America it carries the Zika virus. The insect has spread to North America but has not brought diseases with it—but experts are keeping watch.

Saw-scaled viper

Echis carinatus

 Unlike most snakes, the saw-scaled viper is very aggressive and bites with little warning.

 It strikes so quickly that it may fling itself into the air. This viper sometimes appears in Middle Eastern stories as a flying serpent.

 When warning off animals and people, this little snake does not hiss. Instead, it rubs its ridged scales against each other to make a terrifying rasp. The sound is similar to the sizzling of a frying pan.

Fact file

Lives: Western and southern Asia

Habitat: Deserts and other dry areas

Length: 1–2 ft. (40–60 cm)

Venom dose: 0.1 oz. (0.3 g)

Lifespan: 20 years

Diet: Worms, frogs, toads, lizards, bird eggs

This viper's venom attacks the flesh and blood around a bite. Severe bites can cause extreme swelling and blisters.

A single snake can deliver enough venom in one bite to kill two people.

Females do not lay eggs, but instead give birth to their young. They can have up to 28 babies all at once.

Alligator snapping turtle

Macrochelys temminckii

- Alligator snapping turtles are some of the largest and heaviest river turtles in the world.

- The turtle's hooked beak has one of the strongest bites in the animal kingdom. It can easily slice off a human finger.

- This turtle is well protected. It has a thick, spiky shell, a long, flexible tail covered in scales, and tough, star-shaped "eyelashes" surrounding its eyes.

Fact file

Lives: USA

Habitat: Rivers

Length: 2.75–3.25 ft. (80–100 cm)

Weight: 150–175 lb. (70–80 kg)

Lifespan: 45–70 years

Diet: Fish, snails, worms, frogs, crayfish, other turtles

- The turtle lures prey toward it by wiggling the tip of its tongue, which is red and worm-shaped. When a curious creature comes to take a look, the turtle snaps it up.

- It spends most of its time underwater, surfacing every forty minutes to breathe.

- The turtle occasionally leaves the water to look for mates or a new place to live.

Great white shark

Carcharodon carcharias

- The great white is the largest hunting fish in the world.

- It has a super-sensitive nose that can smell a teaspoon of blood dropped into a swimming pool.

- A great white attacks its prey from behind. Just before it bites, it shuts its eyes to prevent them from getting damaged during the impact.

Great whites take a small bite of their victim first to maim and weaken them.

A shark's snout can detect the electricity produced by living bodies. It uses this sense to find prey in dark water.

These predators, with their streamlined bodies and powerful tails, can travel up to 35 miles per hour (55 kph).

Fact file

Lives: Worldwide

Habitat: Oceans

Length: 15–20 ft. (4.5–6 m)

Weight: 5,000 lb. (2,250 kg)

Lifespan: Up to 60 years

Diet: Fish, seals, birds, whale calves

Black widow spider

Latrodectus hesperus

 The black widow spider is the most venomous spider in North America.

The female black widow's venom is 15 times stronger than a rattlesnake's. However, people rarely die from a spider bite because only a tiny amount of venom gets into the blood.

The female spiders often eat their male partners after mating. The male spider provides ideal nutrition for the eggs. This habit gave the species its name, the black widow.

Fact file

Lives: Western North America

Habitat: Rocky areas

Length of females: 1.5 in. (3.5 cm)

Length of males: 0.5 in. (1.5 cm)

Weight: 0.0035 oz. (1 g)

Lifespan of females: 3 years

Lifespan of males: 6 weeks

Diet: Insects

The females have a distinctive red hourglass shape on the underside of their shiny, black abdomens.

 Females mate with several males in the summer, laying clutches of eggs in silken sacs that hang on their messy webs.

 Each egg sac holds 750 eggs, but a month after hatching, only about 12 spiderlings make it to adulthood. Often, the spiderlings will eat each other!

Gray wolf

Canis lupus

- A group of wolves is called a pack. A pack working together is capable of taking down large animals such as elk and caribou.

- Wolves can spot vulnerable animals in a herd—the old or young, or injured animals. They select these as their prey.

- A wolf pack exhausts its prey with many bites to the legs and face. Once the victim finally collapses, the wolves start eating without waiting for it to die.

- Despite being some of the best hunters in the animal kingdom, wolves rarely attack humans.

Fact file

Lives: North America, Europe, North Africa, Asia

Habitat: Tundra and forest

Length: 2.5–5 ft. (0.75–1.5 m)

Weight: 50–175 lb. (25–80 kg)

Lifespan: 8–13 years

Diet: Moose, deer, caribou, rabbits, rodents

Wolves often appear in fairy stories as cunning and deadly creatures. This view of wolves was probably formed in ancient times, when wolf packs and human hunters competed for food.

Wolf howls can be heard up to 10 miles (16 km) away.

Leopard

Panthera pardus

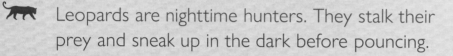 Leopards are nighttime hunters. They stalk their prey and sneak up in the dark before pouncing.

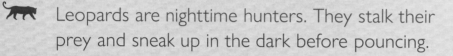 A leopard's spotty coat makes it hard for other animals to see it among trees and long grass.

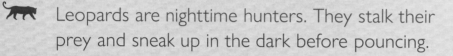 A leopard's ears are five times more sensitive than a human's.

Fact file

Lives: Africa and southern Asia

Habitat: Forest and grasslands

Length: 3.25–6 ft. (1–1.9 m)

Weight: 65–175 lb. (30–80 kg)

Lifespan: 12–17 years

Diet: Antelope, gazelle, deer

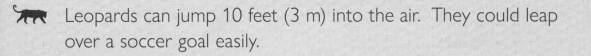 Leopards can jump 10 feet (3 m) into the air. They could leap over a soccer goal easily.

These large cats are incredibly fast. They are capable of running at speeds of 36 miles per hour (58 kph).

Leopards are not fussy eaters. They will hunt nearly anything meaty they encounter, from a little mouse to an adult human.

Leopards use the white spots on the tip of their tail and on the backs of each ear to send signals to other leopards.

Southern cassowary

Casuarius casuarius

 The southern cassowary is thought to be the most dangerous bird in the world.

 By repeatedly kicking downward, the southern cassowary uses its lethal 4.5-inch (12 cm) razor-sharp claws to inflict deep cuts and break bones.

 The southern cassowary cannot fly, but it can run at around 30 miles per hour (50 kph).

Fact file

Lives: New Guinea and northern Australia

Habitat: Rain forest

Height: 4.5–5.5 ft. (1.25–1.75 cm)

Weight: 35–130 lb. (17–60 kg)

Lifespan: 30 years

Diet: Fruits, fungus, insects

The birds live alone and communicate by sending low, booming calls—like roars—through the forest. These calls are the deepest call of any bird, and people can only just hear them.

Cassowaries are powerful swimmers and good jumpers. They have been known to charge and leap feet-first, slashing with their hooked claws.

Deathstalker scorpion

Leiurus quinquestriatus

 The deathstalker's venom is one of the most powerful of any scorpion.

 This scorpion kills prey with its tough pincers, and saves its venom for stinging predators and other threats.

 A sting from a deathstalker is extraordinarily painful but rarely fatal to a healthy adult human. However, small doses can be lethal for children and those with weak hearts.

Fact file

Lives: North Africa and the Middle East

Habitat: Desert

Length: 3–4.25 in. (8–11 cm)

Weight: 0.05–0.1 oz. (1–1.25 g)

Lifespan: 4 years

Diet: Insects, spiders, worms

The deathstalker lies in wait for food. It can sense when prey is approaching from the vibrations of their footsteps.

When food is sparse, these scorpions will resort to cannibalism. In fact, one of their most common predators are deathstalker scorpions!

One of the chemicals found in deathstalker venom, called chlorotoxin, is being developed as a possible drug to treat brain cancer.

Portuguese man-of-war

Physalia physalis

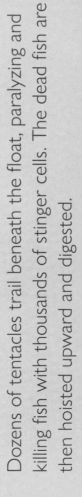

- This ocean stinger is not a single animal but a colony of creatures called siphonophores, which are close relatives of jellyfish.

- Portuguese man-of-wars often travel in swarms of 1,000 individuals. They kill a huge amount of the fish in an area before moving on.

- Dozens of tentacles trail beneath the float, paralyzing and killing fish with thousands of stinger cells. The dead fish are then hoisted upward and digested.

- The curved, sail-like float catches the wind. Sailors named the creature in the 18th century. Its sail reminded them of big Portuguese warships.

Around 10,000 people are stung by Portuguese man-of-wars every year while swimming in the sea. The stings are painful, but not life-threatening.

The 6-inch (15-cm) tall float is filled with carbon monoxide mixed with air. If a bird attacks, the animal lets out the gas and sinks underwater for a while.

Fact file

Lives: Atlantic Ocean

Habitat: Ocean surface

Length, body: 1 ft. (30 cm)

Tentacles: 33–65 ft. (10–20 m)

Lifespan: 1 year

Diet: Fish, shrimp, plankton

Green anaconda

Eunectes murinus

- The green anaconda is the largest snake in the world. Although some Asian pythons grow longer, none can match the weight and width of a big green anaconda.

- The green anaconda is an ambush predator. It lies in wait, then strikes out and grabs its prey in its powerful jaws. It then coils itself around its victim.

- When coiled, the anaconda squeezes until its prey can no longer breathe. Eventually, the victim will suffocate or go into cardiac arrest.

- Anacondas are big enough to kill and eat humans, but these snakes avoid unusual prey and generally slither away from people.

Fact file

Lives: South America

Habitat: Wetland

Length: 20–30 ft. (6–9 m)

Weight: 550 lb. (250 kg)

Lifespan: 30 years

Diet: Deer, caiman, rodents, lizards, birds, fish

The green anaconda can bite. It has many hooked teeth for gripping prey, but it kills by constricting the prey instead.

This big snake has no natural enemies. It preys on anything it can swallow, including caiman and even—very rarely—jaguars.

The anaconda always swallows its prey headfirst. That way, the prey's legs will fold against its body and slide easily into the anaconda's stomach.

Bison

Bison bison

Bison are one of the most dangerous wild animals in North America. They attack around three times as many people as bears.

When spooked, a herd will stampede, galloping at 40 miles per hour (65 kph), devastating anything in its path.

Bison can use their horns to pick up and throw a wolf so high in the air that the fall is enough to kill its unfortunate victim.

Bison have bad eyesight, but they can smell another animal 2 miles (3 km) away.

Fact file

Lives: North America

Habitat: Woodlands and prairie

Length: 7–11.5 ft. (2–3.5 m)

Weight: 800–2,200 lb. (360–1,000 kg)

Lifespan: 15–20 years

Diet: Grass

Bulls born early in the year will grow bigger than males calves that arrived later, and be more dominant for their whole lives. The biggest bulls race to breed early each year so their sons will also be big and powerful.

Orca

Orcinus orca

Orcas are huge predators that eat up to 375 pounds (170 kg) of food every day.

A pod, or group, of orcas is a deadly hunting team. Working together, they can kill anything from great white sharks to whale calves.

Different orca pods specialize in hunting certain animals. Some attack seals, some eat only fish, and others prey on whales.

These powerful predators use 4-inch (10-cm) long teeth to feast on marine mammals.

Orcas are highly intelligent mammals. An orca's brain is five times bigger than a human's.

An orca's bite strength has never been measured, but the size of its jaw and muscles suggests it has the most powerful bite of any animal—at least twice as strong as a crocodiles.

Orcas use their great strength to tip over ice floes where seals are resting. The seals plunge into the water and cannot escape.

Fact file

Lives: Worldwide

Habitat: Cold oceans

Length: 30 ft. (9 m)

Weight: 15,000 lb. (7,200 kg)

Lifespan: 70 years

Diet: Fish, squid, birds, seals, whales

Dyeing poison frog

Dendrobates tinctorius

- Dyeing poison frogs are among the most brightly colored, poisonous frogs found in South America.

- The frog's bright colors are a warning to predators that eating it will make them sick.

- This little frog eats ants and other insects. Most of its prey is poisonous, but the frog is unaffected. The frog takes the poison from its food and adds it to its skin.

- Simply touching this frog's skin will transfer powerful poison into the bloodstream, but in amounts too small to harm humans.

Fact file

Lives: Brazil, French Guiana, Guyana, Suriname

Habitat: Rain forest

Length: 1.25–2.5 in. (3–6 cm)

Weight: 0.1–0.25 oz. (3–8 g)

Lifespan: 5 years

Diet: Insects and spiders

Local people in Suriname collect the poison from several species of frogs and use it to make deadly hunting arrows.

Female frogs lay one egg at a time on a clean leaf. The male guards the egg, and when the tadpole hatches, he carries it to a little pool in between the leaves of lush forest plants.

The female visits the pool every few days, and lays an unfertilized egg in it for her tadpole to eat.

Dyeing poison frogs raised in captivity do not develop poison, but those in the wild are among the most poisonous animals in the world.

Funnel-web spider

Atrax robustus

 This small, dark creature has one of the most powerful venoms of any spider. It delivers the venom through its stabbing fangs.

 After biting an animal or human, the spider's long, widely spaced fangs often get stuck in the skin, and the spider has to be flicked off.

 When a funnel-web spider bites a human, it is always a medical emergency and it has to be treated as quickly as possible.

 The venom has very powerful effects on the human nervous system and on other primates, monkeys and apes in particular.

Fact file

Lives: Eastern Australia

Habitat: Rocky forests, logs, compost heaps

Length of female: 1.5 in. (3.5 cm)

Length of male: 1 in. (2.5 cm)

Lifespan: 8 years

Diet: Insects, snails, frogs

It is usually males that bite humans. They spend much of their time roaming around looking for mates and are very aggressive when disturbed.

Funnel-web spiders are nocturnal and sensitive to sunlight, and can be found hiding in shoes during the daytime. Australians living in the countryside learn to check their shoes for spiders!

Tiger

Panthera tigris

- A tiger can kill an animal that weighs four times its own weight.

- A tiger kills one or two animals each week. It buries the leftovers to eat later.

- Each tiger controls a huge territory—about 25 to 40 square miles (60–100 sq. km).

- Tigers mark their territory with claw marks scraped into trees and rocks.

- Tigers kill their prey by biting their victims' necks so that they cannot breathe. They use their body weight to push the victim to the ground.

Fact file

Lives: Southern and eastern Asia

Habitat: Forests and swamps

Length: 6.5–10.5 ft. (2–3.25 m)

Weight: 225–675 lb. (100–300 kg)

Lifespan: 12–15 years

Diet: Deer, cattle, pigs

These nighttime predators use their coats as camouflage. They prey on buffalo, deer, moose, and other large animals.

Older tigers prey on humans when they are too weak to catch larger prey, or when their usual prey supply has dwindled.

Tigers have a tremendous leaping ability, capable of jumping about 25 to 30 feet (8–10 m).

Black mamba

Dendroaspis polylepis

🐍 The black mamba is the longest venomous snake in Africa.

🐍 A bite from a black mamba is fatally venomous and can kill a person in just twenty minutes. Before an antivenin was found, a bite would almost always result in death.

🐍 The black mamba is one of the fastest snakes on Earth. It can slither along at 12.5 miles per hour (20 kph).

🐍 The snake moves on the rear two-thirds of its body, holding the front third above the ground to spot prey.

Fact file

Lives: Southern and eastern Africa

Habitat: Grasslands, rocky hills, and riverside forests

Length: 6.5–14 ft. (2–4.25 m)

Weight: 3.5 lb. (1.5 kg)

Lifespan: 11 years

Diet: Eggs, birds, young snakes, frogs, lizards, small mammals

Male mambas often fight over mates. They coil their bodies around each other in contests of strength.

The snake is mostly greenish brown, but it gets its name from the blue-black lining of its mouth, which is revealed when the snake gives a menacing hiss.

The mamba is easily recognizable. The mouth curves into a smile on the sides of its box-shaped head.

Polar bear

Ursus maritimus

🐻 Polar bears are the world's largest land predator.

🐻 A polar bear's diet consists mostly of seals, but when food is scarce it will eat almost anything.

🐻 Polar bears have a keen sense of smell. They can pick up a scent up to about 0.5 miles (1 km) away and can even smell through ice 3 feet (1m) thick.

🐻 These bears have strong, sharp claws that they use for hunting and digging through snow. Each paw has five thick, curved claws up to 6 inches (15 cm) long.

Fact file

Lives: Arctic Ocean

Habitat: Ice and tundra

Length: 8–10 ft. (2.5–3 m)

Weight: 775–1,550 lb. (350–700 kg)

Lifespan: 15–18 years

Diet: Seals, fish, deer, berries

They use their great weight to break through ice to reach prey underneath. The bears rear up on their back legs and then smash downward with their front paws.

Polar bears spend the summer at sea—walking on the frozen ocean or swimming for up to about 60 miles (100 km) to find food.

Komodo dragon

Varanus komodoensis

- The Komodo dragon is the largest and heaviest lizard on Earth. This dangerous predator has a flat head, scaly skin, and a huge, muscular tail.

- This giant lizard only lives on the island of Komodo and a few other small islands in Indonesia.

- The Komodo dragon is the largest and fiercest predator on these islands. It has no natural enemies and would attack a person if they came too close.

- The lizard can sprint for a short distance but is too slow to chase most prey. Instead, it creeps up on them and attacks by surprise.

This hunter has venom mixed into its spit. When it bites prey, the venom goes into the victim's blood and kills it gradually.

As top predators, they will eat anything from deer and pigs to large water buffalo. Rotting carrion will do if there's nothing else.

Komodo dragons are cannibals. The bigger adults eat baby Komodo dragons and sometimes other adults, too.

Fact file

Lives: Komodo and surrounding islands (Indonesia)

Habitat: Woodland

Length: 6.6–10 ft. (2–3 m)

Weight: 150–200 lb. (70–90 kg)

Lifespan: 30 years

Diet: Mammals and carrion

Asian giant hornet

Vespa mandarinia

 This stinging insect is the largest hornet in the world. In Japan it is known as the giant sparrow bee.

 The hornet has a 0.25-inch (6 mm) stinger on its rear end. Its sting is so deep and painful that people refer to the insect as a yak killer.

Giant hornets live in underground colonies. They raid honeybee hives, eventually taking them over.

The giant hornet is twenty times heavier than a worker honeybee.

Fact file

Lives: Eastern and southeast Asia

Habitat: Forests

Length: 1.25–2 in. (3.5–5.5 cm)

Wingspan: 1.25–3 in. (3.5–7.5 cm)

Lifespan: 3 months

Diet: Beetles, wasps, bees

One hornet sting is harmless, but if you are stung more than ten times, you should see a doctor. Receiving thirty stings is a medical emergency, and sixty or more is nearly always fatal.

 In Japan, about forty people die of hornet stings every year. This is the most dangerous animal in the country.

 This huge hornet can fly at speeds of up to 25 miles per hour (40 kph), which is faster than people can run.

Lion's mane jellyfish

Cyanea capillata

 The lion's mane jellyfish is the largest jellyfish in the world.

It can have up to 1,200 tentacles hanging from its bell-shaped body. Tentacles are divided into eight clusters, with 150 tentacles on each cluster.

These manelike clusters give this jellyfish its name.

 Their tentacles are covered in tiny stingers that fire poisoned spikes into anything they touch.

 The tentacles can trail 120 feet (37 m) into the water—which is longer than a blue whale!

The jellyfish extend their tentacles outward to create a trap, catching and killing fish and other prey with their poisonous needle-like stingers.

 Once caught, the fish and other prey are slowly pulled up the tentacles and into the mouth.

Fact file

Lives: North Atlantic, North Pacific, and Arctic oceans

Habitat: Cold waters

Width: 7.5 ft. (2.25 m)

Weight: 2,200 lb. (1,000 kg)

Lifespan: 1 year

Diet: Fish and shrimp

Geography cone snail

Conus geographus

- Sea snails have some of the deadliest venom on Earth. Of over 500 cone snail species, this species is the most dangerous.

- The venom contains 200 chemicals, and each sting includes enough venom to kill fifteen people. The poisons make people feel numb, and without medical help, they would eventually stop breathing.

- As little as 70 millionths of a gram of the venom can kill a person.

- The cone snail venom makes their fish prey go stiff, making them easier to swallow whole.

Fact file

Lives: Indian and eastern Pacific oceans

Habitat: Seabed

Length: 2.75–6 in. (7–15 cm)

Weight: 0.5–2 oz. (15–60 g)

Lifespan: 3 years

Diet: Fish

The snail uses its venom to kill its prey, harpooning them with a sharp tongue that shoots out from the shell.

There is no cure for cone snail venom. If a person gets to a hospital fast enough, doctors will use machines to keep them alive and wait until the venom wears off.

One chemical in the venom is being tested as a painkiller. If it's found to be safe, it will be 10,000 times more powerful than the most common drugs used today.

White rhinoceros

Ceratotherium simum

 Rhinos are huge, fast, and extremely dangerous mammals. They don't go looking for trouble, but if anything comes too close, they will quickly become very aggressive.

Rhinos have very bad eyesight and attack anything that gets in their way, including cars, hikers, and even tree stumps. Even a friendly visitor might spook a rhino!

Male rhinos can charge at a speed of 40 miles per hour (65 kph), which is much faster than a person can run.

Fact file

Lives: Africa

Habitat: Grassy savannah

Length: 12.5–16.5 ft. (3.8–5 m)

Weight: 4,000–6,000 lb. (1,800–2,700 kg)

Lifespan: 40–50 years

Diet: Grass

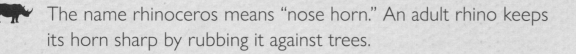 The name rhinoceros means "nose horn." An adult rhino keeps its horn sharp by rubbing it against trees.

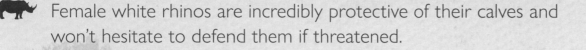 Female white rhinos are incredibly protective of their calves and won't hesitate to defend them if threatened.

A white rhino's skin is gray-brown; the white in their name may have come from a word for wide, referring to their wide mouths, but people are still unsure about this.

Rhinos are very rare because they are hunted for their horns, which some cultures use in traditional medicines.

Tiger shark

Galeocerdo cuvier

- Since records began, tiger sharks have killed about 100 people, and attacked many more.

- The tiger shark gets its name from the spots and stripes on the skin of young sharks. These markings fade away by adulthood.

- Tiger sharks swim slowly, which makes them harder to see in murky water. They then make their attack with a final, high-speed surge.

Dolphins usually ignore most sharks, but they will vacate an area very quickly if they spot a tiger shark.

Tiger sharks are sometimes called the "garbage cans of the sea" because they eat just about anything, including car tires, oil cans, and license plates.

Tiger sharks are sometimes attacked and eaten by pods of orcas, or killer whales.

Fact file

Lives: Worldwide

Habitat: Warm coastal waters

Length: 10–18 ft. (3–5.5 m)

Weight: 900–2,000 lb. (408–907 kg)

Lifespan: 15–40 years

Diet: Fish, squid, jellyfish, seabirds, sea turtles

Snow leopard

Panthera uncia

- Of all the big cats, snow leopards are the only species that cannot roar.

- Snow leopards prey on mountain animals like goats and ground squirrels. They are capable of killing prey three times their own weight.

- The snow leopard's smoky-gray camouflage is so effective that it is known as the ghost cat. The leopard's spots get paler in winterso it can hide better among the snow-covered rocks.

- Snow leopards have huge, furry paws that spread their weight evenly across snow and muffle the sound of their movement, allowing them to sneak up on their prey unnoticed.

- This mountain leopard holds the animal long-jump record. It can leap about 50 feet (15 m)—the length of a bus.

- This cat can climb two-thirds of the way up Mount Everest, making it the highest hunting mammal in the world.

Fact file

Lives: Central Asia

Habitat: Mountains

Length: 3.25–5 ft. (1–1.5 m)

Weight: 75–120 lb. (35–55 kg)

Lifespan: 10 years

Diet: Sheep, goats, deer, small mammals like marmots

King cobra

Ophiophagus hannah

- Also known as the hamadryad, the king cobra is the longest venomous snake in the world.

- This huge snake rises up and opens the hood around its neck to scare away animals that come too close. Unlike other snakes, its hiss sounds like a low growl.

- A king cobra can lift the first third of its body off the ground and look an adult human in the eye.

- One bite from this snake contains enough venom to kill an elephant. The venom attacks the nerves and breathing systems of prey. Luckily, bites on humans are quite rare.

Fact file

Lives: India, southeast Asia

Habitat: Forest

Length: 8–18 ft. (2.5–5.5 m)

Weight: 13 lb. (6 kg)

Lifespan: 17 years

Diet: Mainly snakes, also lizards, small mammals

The cobra preys mostly on other snakes—including pythons and venomous snakes—as well as lizards and some mammals. It is immune to the venom from other snakes.

Female king cobras bury their eggs under rotting leaves and sit guard on top of them, not eating for weeks. At this time, the giant snake is at its most dangerous, attacking anyone that comes too close.

Just before her eggs hatch, the mother snake slithers away. She is so hungry that she needs to find food quickly to avoid eating her own babies!

Electric eel

Electrophorus electricus

- Despite its name, this species is a knifefish, not an eel.

- The fish stuns its prey and scares off threats by giving them powerful electric shocks. River animals quickly learn to stay away from an electric eel.

- About 80 percent of the animal's body is made up of organs that create the electrical charge. The stomach, heart, and all other organs are crammed into the front 20 percent of the body.

- The head of the fish is positively charged, while the tail is negative. By touching its victim with both ends of its body, the electric eel creates a surge of electricity that zaps its victim.

- The electric shock is about 860 volts. The electricity in homes is between 120 and 250 volts.

- Despite the high charge, the fish's shock lasts just 2 milliseconds, which is not enough to kill a person.

- Human deaths are extremely rare. However, shocks are strong enough to stun, and people may drown as a result.

- Electric eels are nocturnal and hunt in muddy water. They use electrical detectors in the skin to pick up the movements of prey in the dark.

- When threatened from land, these eels will leap from water to stun potential predators, including people.

Fact file

Lives: South America

Habitat: Riverbeds

Length: 6.5 ft. (2 m)

Weight: 45 lb. (20 kg)

Lifespan: 20 years

Diet: Fish

Striped hyena

Hyaena hyaena

- Striped hyenas have incredibly powerful muscles in their very wide jaws. They can crack through bone with their teeth.

- Hyenas have one of the strongest bite forces in the world. It is stronger than both a lion's and a tiger's.

- When it is ready to fight, a hyena raises the hair around its neck. This makes it look biggerand tougher.

- These predators will chase their prey, overpowering it with powerful bites to legsand soft belly.

- These animals give out a chuckling call when nervous to warn others to stay away.

Fact file

Lives: Africa, Asia

Habitat: Grasslands, woodlands

Length: 3.25 ft. (1 m)

Weight: 50–90 lb. (25–40 kg)

Lifespan: 12 years

Diet: Carrion, fruit, insects

Striped hyenas are mainly solitary, or live in small groups where the female is in charge.

In the Serengeti, striped hyenas walk for an average of 12 miles (about 20 km) each night looking for food.

Siafu ants

Dorylus species

- The word siafu means "ants" in Swahili, which is the main language spoken in East Africa.

- A siafu ant queen lays 4 million eggs every month.

- These ants spend a lot of time on the move, traveling over the ground in long columns of around 50 million individuals. They are also known as driver ants.

- The smaller worker ants walk in the middle of the column, while the larger soldier ants, which are equipped with powerful, pincerlike jaws, march along the edges.

- The ants defend themselves by biting and stinging.

Fact file

Lives: Africa and Asia

Habitat: Rain forest and savannah

Length of a worker ant:
  0.1 in (2.5 mm)

Length of a soldier ant:
  0.3 in (7.5 mm)

Lifespan of a queen: 5 years

Diet: Insects and carrion

All siafu ants are blind. They use scent messages called pheromones to communicate with each other about where to go, when to feed, and when an attack might be coming.

The column attacks anything in its path. It can only move around 20 meters per hour (0.01 mph) so is fairly easy to escape from. However, if a person cannot run away, the ants will eat them.

In the wild, soldier siafu ants can be used to stitch up bad cuts. The ants bite on both sides of the wound, pulling it closed. If the ant's body is removed, the pincer mouth will stay shut like a staple.

Lionfish

Pterois volitans

- The lionfish is also called the turkeyfish, because its long, spiked fins look like bird feathers.

- The hollow spines on the back of the fish inject venom into predators that try to bite it.

- Lionfish use their camouflage and quick reflexes to ambush prey quickly, opening its mouth to suck in its meal whole.

- A lionfish sting hurts, but it is not lethal to humans. Divers can get stung by accident when swimming in reefs. Hot water will destroy the poison and stop the pain.

- When threatened, the lionfish swims with its head down so the poisonous spines face its attacker.

- Lionfish are cannibals and will eat each other if there is no other food around.

Fact file

Lives: Indian and western Pacific oceans

Habitat: Rocky reefs

Length: 16 in. (40 cm)

Weight: 3 lb. (1.3 kg)

Lifespan: 10 years

Diet: Crabs and fish

Nile crocodile

Crocodylus niloticus

- This African crocodile has one of the strongest bites of any land animal—about 25 times stronger than that of a human.

- Despite having huge muscles to shut its mouth, the crocodile's muscles for opening its mouth are very weak. A human could hold the crocodile's mouth closed with their hands.

- This crocodile cannot chew its food, so instead, it swallows small meals whole. It twists off chunks of meat from larger prey by gripping onto the animal and rolling around to dislodge the meat.

- The Nile crocodile can go for weeks without food. It saves energy between meals by lying still on riverbanks.

- This crocodile can gallop over land faster than a human can run, but only for short distances.

- They do most of their hunting in shallow waters. They swim close to the bank and grab animals with their mouths, pulling victims under the water until they drown.

- Their crushing bite is enough to capture a lion. If the big cat is taken by surprise while pausing for a drink, the Nile crocodile can pull it into the water.

Fact file

Lives: Africa, Madagascar

Habitat: Rivers, lakes, swamps

Length: 11–20 ft. (3.5–6 m)

Weight: 500–2,500 lb. (225–1,100 kg)

Lifespan: 100 years

Diet: Fish, mammals, birds

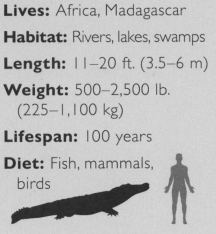

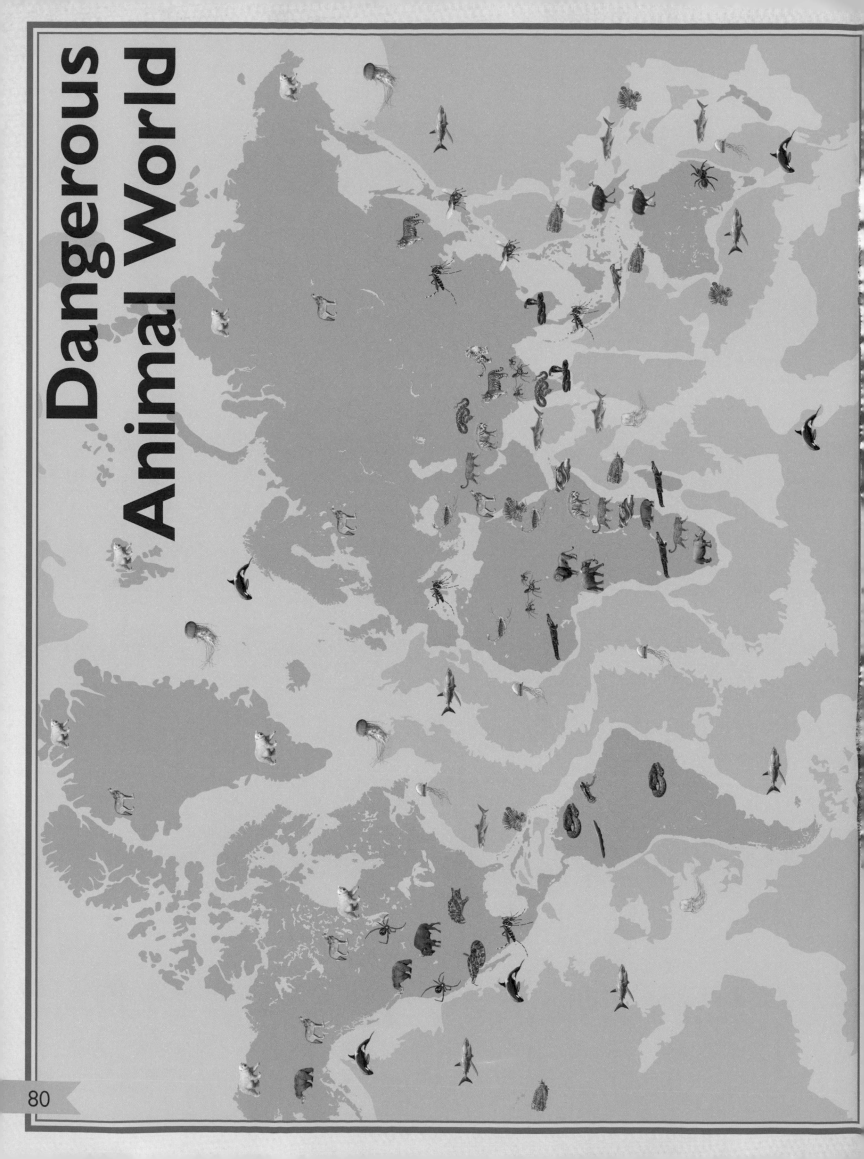

Dangerous Animal World